RELIGIONS OF THE WORLD

I Am Protestant

❧ PHILEMON D. SEVASTIADES ❧

The Rosen Publishing Group's
PowerKids Press
New York

Published in 1996 by The Rosen Publishing Group, Inc.
29 East 21st Street, New York, NY 10010

First Edition

Photo credits: Cover photo © Barbara Ureye/International Stock; p. 4 © Cindy Reiman/Impact Visuals; p. 7 © Suzanne A. Viamis/International Stock; p. 8 © Lester Sloan/Gamma Liaison; p. 11 © Peter Russell Clemens/International Stock; p. 12 by Philemon D. Sevastiades; p. 15 © Mark Bolster/International Stock; p. 16 © Stacy Rosenstock/Impact Visuals; p. 19 © Jim Levitt/Impact Visuals; p.20 © Bill Stanton/International Stock.

Sevastiades, Philemon.
    I am Protestant / Philemon Sevastiades.— 1st ed.
      p.   cm.— (Religions of the world)
    Includes index.
    Summary: Introduces some basic tenets of Protestant religions.
    ISBN 0-8239-2378-9
     1. Protestant churches—Doctrines—Juvenile literature.[1. Protestant churches—doctrines.]
     I. Title. II. Series: Religions of the world (Rosen Publishing Group)
BX4811.S48 1996
280'.4—dc20

96-1941
CIP
AC

Manufactured in the United States of America

Contents

Being Protestant

My name is Yvonne. I live in Atlanta. I am a Protestant Christian. There are many different kinds of Protestant Christians. There are many religions that call themselves Protestant. All of these religions believe in Jesus Christ. We all call ourselves Christians. My parents are **Evangelical** (ee-van-JEL-i-kul). My uncle is **Presbyterian** (prez-bit-TEER-ee-an). Both of these religions are Protestant. My brother and I go to church with my parents.

◀ *All Protestants believe in Jesus Christ.*

Jesus Christ

We believe that Jesus Christ is God. We also believe that he is the Son of God. We call him our Lord and **Savior** (SAVE-your). We call him Lord because we believe that he is the ruler of all things. We call him Savior because we believe that he has saved us from **spiritual** (SPEER-i-chu-all) death and sin. Sins are acts and thoughts that displease God.

Protestants believe that Jesus is God and the Son of God. ▶

Prayer

My family and I pray many times during the day. We pray together in the morning. At breakfast, we give thanks for the food, and pray for God's guidance throughout the day. In the evenings, we pray and read the Bible together. We take turns. My mom or dad explains the meaning of the stories to us. Our **pastor** (PASS-tur) or **minister** (MIN-i-stur) says that we should pray whenever we feel the need for God's help and comfort.

◀ *Many Protestants pray both in church and at home.*

Christmas and Easter

At Christmas we celebrate the birth of Jesus Christ. It is my favorite time of year. Christmas is a happy and joyful time. We put up a tree in our house. We go to church on Christmas day and sing Christmas carols. At Easter, we remember that Jesus died for our sins. We believe that he rose from the dead. We believe that he will come again soon to decide who will go to heaven.

Like all Christians, Protestants celebrate the birth of Jesus at Christmas. ▶

The Bible

We believe that the Bible is the word of God. My father says that in the Old Testament, God promised to send us his son, Jesus, to save our **souls** (SOLES). In the New Testament, there are four books about Jesus and his life. There are also letters written by some of his followers. These tell us about what we believe and what God expects of us. That is why my family studies the Bible every day.

◄ *The Bible gives examples of how God wants Christians to live their lives.*

Sin

Our pastor teaches us that sin is bad. When we do things that are hurtful to others or to ourselves, God is not pleased with us. My dad and mom try to teach me what is good. They use examples from the Bible. We believe that only Jesus can forgive our sins. If we are forgiven, then we will please God while we live, and we will go to heaven when we die.

Parents help their children understand how to be good and please God. ▶

The Spirit

We believe that the Spirit is God's presence in the world. We believe that the Spirit lives in us, guiding us and teaching us in our daily lives. The Spirit can make **miracles** (MEER-i-kulz) happen. God's spirit, the Holy Spirit, can help us understand God and his son, Jesus Christ.

◀ *Protestants believe that God's spirit guides them.*

Being Saved

My mom says that being saved means knowing that we will go to heaven one day. It is part of our personal relationship with Jesus Christ. I have accepted Jesus as my personal savior. That means that I have a special relationship with him. So do my mom, dad, brother, and sisters. Some people call that being "born again."

Accepting Jesus as their personal savior is a powerful experience for many people. ▶

Baptism

My brother, Jeff, is ten years old. At our church, Jeff accepted Jesus as his personal savior. This means that he can be **baptized** (BAP-tized) now. All the people in the church will gather around him and pray for him. The pastor will dip his whole body in water. It is a happy time for us.

◄ *Various Protestant religions baptize at different ages. Lutherans, for example, baptize infants.*

21

Going to Church

My family and I go to church on Sundays and at least once during the week. We read from the Bible, and the pastor leads us in prayers. The most important part of our service is when the pastor gives the sermon. A sermon is a talk based on part of the Bible. It is about something in our lives and teaches us how to act. We also sing lots of songs about Jesus. These are called hymns.

Glossary

baptism (BAP-tizm) Ceremony showing that someone has become part of a Christian religion.

Evangelical (ee-van-JEL-i-kul) One of many Protestant religions.

minister (MIN-i-stur) Religious leader.

miracle (MEER-i-kul) Something that is impossible but that happens anyway.

pastor (PASS-tur) Religious leader.

Presbyterian (prez-bit-TEER-ee-an) One of many Protestant religions.

Savior (SAVE-your) Jesus Christ, who makes sure that those who are saved have a place in heaven.

soul (SOLE) The part of yourself that goes to heaven.

spiritual (SPEER-i-chu-all) Dealing with the soul rather than with the body.

23

Index